PADLOCKS AND
GIRDLES OF
CHASTITY

PADLOCKS AND GIRDLES

OF CHASTITY

FREDONIA BOOKS
Amsterdam. The Netherlands

Padloscks and Girdles of Chastity

by
Alcide Bonneau

ISBN: 1-58963-347-4

Reprinted from the original edition

Fredonia Books
Amsterdam, The Netherlands
http://www.fredoniabooks.com

In order to make original editions of historical works
available to scholars at an economical price, this
facsimile of the original edition is reproduced from
the best available copy and has been digitally
enhanced to improve legibility, but the text remains
unaltered to retain historical authenticity.

PADLOCKS AND
GIRDLES OF
CHASTITY

INTRODUCTION

You may see, if you will, the origin of padlocks of chastity in that peculiar knot, called the Herculean knot, which used to fasten the woolen sash of the Grecian maiden, and which the husband alone was to untie on his

wedding night. Solidify this knot, apply it
to iron bars, and you have almost the padlock. But the Greeks do not appear to have
been acquainted with this safety-apparatus.
It is only in Voltaire's story that we see
Prosperpine defended by an armour of this
kind. Vulcan, the able artisan, never suc-
ceeded but in forging the famous net which
enabled him to catch people in the very act,
though not to prevent them. And when
Ulysses used to fasten the door of his royal
house with a peg driven into straps, he
would have doubtless been at a great loss to
put a lock on Penelope.

The girdle of virginity, worn by the
Grecian maidens, used to be put on at the
nubile age and taken off after marriage;
quite on the contrary, the girdle of chastity
was presented by the husband to the wife
in the morning of his wedding-night, as a
most suitable means of maintaining union
and good understanding between them, by
dispelling all his jealous fears. We see in
the pseudo-Meursius's *Aloysia,* that elegant
picture of the morals of the 16th century,
with what arguments a husband, who has
good grounds for being on his guard, persuades his wife to put one on; it is herself,

Tullia, who relates the incident to her friend Ottavia: "Truly," said he, "I am fully persuaded that thou art exceedingly honest and chaste; yet I fear for thy virtue unless we both come to its aid."—"What act, what fault have I committed to put such an idea into thy head, my heart?" I asked; "what opinion hast thou formed of me? Withal, I do not wish to depreciate any scheme thou mayst have fostered." — "I want," said he, "to put a girdle of chastity on thee; if thou art chaste, thou wilt not be annoyed at it; why, if not, it is thy business to see how right I am in doing what I propose." — "I will put on me whatever thou choosest," I replied; "be it what it may, I shall gladly wear it, as I was born to be thine: I shall heartily be a wife for only thee and live isolated from the rest of men, whom I despise and detest. I shall neither speak to Lampridio nor look at him." — "Don't act thus," said he; "on the contrary, I wish thee to act friendly and decently with him, so that neither he nor I may have any reason to complain of thee: he, in case thou didst treat him too rudely, and I, shouldst thou make too free with him. But the girdle of chastity will permit thee to live at greater

liberty with him, whilst offering me full
security on the side of Lampridio." Then
with a silk ribbon which he placed round
my body above the hips, he measured the
size the girdle should be round the thick part
of my body; with another ribbon, he took
the measure of the space from my groins to
my hips. This done: "Even in this matter,"
said he, "I shall try and let thee see how
greatly I esteem thee. The little chains,
which are to be overlaid with velveting, will
be of gold; the portcullis will be of gold,
the gold opening will be studded over with
precious stones. The most famous gold-
smith of our town will, as he is under great
obligations to me, set to work at it that it
may be a master-piece of his art. I shall be
but conferring an honor upon thee, while
seeming to be doing thee wrong."[1]

---

1)　Nicolas Chorier's *Dialogues of Luisa Sigea;* English
edition, Paris Lise-ux, 1890, Dialogue V, p. 100.

11

Monsieur de Laborde [2] seems, however, to be of opinion that the specimens now extant of those tools are devoid of authenticity. "Forced interpretation," says he, "have given a tale a sort of legal existence,

---

2) *Notice de émaux du Louvre*, tome II, *Glossaire;* art. *Ceinture de chasteté.*

and several to recommend curious collections belonging to amateurs' museums. These girdles have not existed as the current fashion, especially in so sprightly a nation as ours; they may have been exceptionally invented, as the whim of some maniac. I reject them, therefore, and advise amateurs to do so likewise." Nobody pretends that such a practice has existed among any European people as a general custom, or current fashion; but the husbands and jealous lovers, who have thought proper to compel their wives or mistresses to put on girdles of chastity in Spain, Italy and even in France, were perhaps more numerous than people imagine. Whatever Molière may have said on this matter, those bolts and gratings are really very efficacious obstacles; their efficacy would be much greater still if this lockwork were applied not only to the doors and windows, but also to the woman's own person, making her thus invulnerable by art. Woman's body is like the larder of man's pleasures, in a selfish point of view; what can be more natural than to padlock the larder, for fear some intruder should come and fall upon the best morsels and eat up the dainties?

The frailty of woman is so well known, ever since Eve and her adventure with the Serpent, that man, in all times and countries, has been trying in every way and sometimes in very cruel ways, to remedy it, without ever believing he is completely safe.   In

regions where the passions are as burning
as the climate, infibulation is one of the
measures to which people had recourse in
olden times, in order to secure the fidelity
of the women and the virginity of the girls.
Strabo speaks of it as of a custom pretty
common among the Ethiopians. De Pauw [1]
distinguishes three sorts of them; but the
learned Dutchman obviously miscalls very
different processes by the same name; the
buckle or fibule is not used in two of these.
"As soon as a girl is born in Ethiopia," says
he, "the lips of her privy parts are united
and sewed together with a silk string, and
there is left in them only the bare opening
that the natural gush requires. You may
imagine what pain a stitching made in so
sensible a spot must cause the victims of
such a monstrous operation. The flesh of
both sides, thus united by art, at length ad-
heres naturally; and towards the second
year, there remains no more but an ugly
seam. The father of a child like this is convinced he has a virgin; and he sells her for
a virgin to him that bids most, as they do
throughout the East. The closed-up parts

_____

[1]   *Recherches philosophiques sur les Américains*, tome
II, p. 140 (Berlin, 1779, 3 vols. 12mo).

are opened again, some time before the girl's marriage, by an incision deep enough to be able to undo the consolidation formed by the sewing.

"As this manner of infibulating is the most frightful and cruel, it is likewise the least in use. In some other tribes of Asia and Africa, they run a ring through the tips of the opposite nymphs; and this ring is so enchased in girls, that it can be removed only by filing it, or by forcibly cutting it with scissors. We imagine that those shackles can be welded only by a soldering, so as to unite both branches of the buckle after it has been sunk into the flesh; and this soldering can be performed only with a red-hot iron, which is laid on the buckle itself, in order to melt in the ore lead. As to the women, they wear there an iron circle provided with a lock, the key of which the husband holds; for this tool supplies the place of seraglio and eunuchs, who require such expense and who cost so dear in Asia, that absolutely nobody but seignors and princes have slaves trained for guarding other slaves; villains from among the populace use those rings we have just spoken about.

"The third manner of infibulating, though not so blood-coloured as the others, is still a horrid relic of barbarity. It consists in putting a girdle of plaited brass wires on women, padlocked above the hips with a lock composed of movable rings, on which they have carved a certain number of characters or figures between which there is but one combination possible for pressing the spring of the padlock, and this combination is the husband's secret."

The first mode of infibulation, which De Pauw had better call by its right name *suture*, is still used in Egypt and among a few negro tribes. Vivant Denon relates that when the Arabs fled at the approach of the French army, in the environs of Syena, the latter found quite little girls with their privy parts sewed, in the abandoned villages. According to more recent travellers, the operation is practiced at the age of eight or nine; and it is no uncommon thing for even married women to be subjected to it. When a Nubian goes on a journey or far-distant expedition, he makes sure in this way that his wife will not suffer herself to be consoled for his absence; skillful matrons are called in to perform the operation at his

departure and the counter-operation at his
return. But we are assured that conjugal
fidelity is not kept any better for this; that
the woman does not hesitate to get herself
ripped up in order to receive her lover;
'tis but getting sewed again, however painful for her, as soon as she hears from some
caravan of her husband's near return. [1]

---

[1]   De Cadalvène, *Egypte et Nubie,* tome II, p. 158.

3

As to infibulation properly so called, it seems to have passed from Egypt and Asia to Rome towards the latter days of the Republic; but, strange to say, it was in order to be applied to men and not to women, and specially to young lads, singers and players.

Celsus (*Medicina,* VII, xxv, 3) has described
for us this little surgical operation: the
prepuce used to be drawn over the glands
of the organ which was forced backwards,
and there used to be a puncture made with a
needle in the two opposite lips. At first, a
thread was introduced into the puncture;
both ends of it were tied and care was taken
to have it slipped every day that it might
not adhere. The healing over, they came
and welded the fibule, which was sometimes of gold, but most frequently of silver:
"*Ad transitum virilitatis custodiuntur agen-
to,*" says *Pliny* (xxxiii, 12), when speaking
of lads. These used to be infibulated at the
stormy time of puberty, so as to preserve
them from premature excesses, and above
all from masturbation; players and singers,
in order to keep their voices from becom-
ing hoarse. As this buckle was very cumbersome, those who used to wear it would
slip it with the yard into a woolen sheath
(*theca*), which was also called by extension
fibule, and which a bandage in the style of
our *suspensories* used to sustain. In fact,
it was a kind of girdle of chastity for the
use of the stronger sex; and it sufficed to
wear one to make people believe that the

wearer was provided with the fibule. Martial tells us of the misadventure that befell Menophilus with respect to this matter:

So far was he from being unprepuced, that his prepuce stuck rivetted for good and all above the glands; but the poor fellow used to wear a huge sheath, to make people believe it was designed for dissembling the biggest of all fibules; the bandage having got loose while he was acting, the truth of the matter became manifest. Every scholar is acquainted with the numerous passages of Pliny, Seneca, Juvenal and Martial, in which there is question of the buckle of the players, the frenzy of love with which the Roman ladies would run after those infibulati, whom their forced continence, they fancied, must make indefatigable athletes in the lists of Venus; and of the great sums of money that these or their masters would extort from those ladies before they would let the fibule be broken. Women who had

---

So huge a fibule clad the yard of Menophilus,
That it alone would have done all the players;
I should have thought, as we often bathe together,
That, being uneasy about his voice, he was caring it in
    this way:
While he was exercising in the palestra, before the eyes
    of all,
Lo the fibule falls of the wretch: he was circumcised!
                                                (VII, 81).

favourite slaves they were jealous of would
get them infibulated also for the same reason; it was more decidedly they that would
have required to be solidly buckled!

The third manner of infibulation described by De Pauw is no other than the
girdle of chastity much the same as we
know it; and, though travellers have lit
upon specimens of it even to the Archipe-
lago of Moluccas, yet their structure and
combinations complicated with padlocks
with letters and figures afford but little room
to see in them inventions of primeval
nations.

The most antique personage in Europe, of
whom history, or rather legend makes men-
tion as having put an apparatus of this kind
on his wives or mistresses, is Francesco II
da Carrara, the last sovereign lord of Padua,
in the 14th century. Freydier, who miscalls
him imperial "viguier," deems him not less
improperly the inventor of it. He had taken
his information from Abbé Misson who
states in his *Journey to Italy* (tome I, p. 112),
that he has been the bust of this tyrant in
the Ducal Palace of Venice. "This tyrant,"
he adds, "who was so remarkable for his
cruelties, and who was strangled with his

four children and his brother by order of
the Senate of Venice. They further show
a little dressing-chest containing six *robinets*
set with springs tted in such a way, that,
on opening the chest these little cannons
went off and killed a lady, Countess Sacrati,
to whom Carrara had sent it as a present.
They show besides small pocket cross-
bows and steel arrows with which he used
to delight in killing those he met, before
they were rightly aware of the blow, or of
him that gave it. *Ibi etiam sunt seroe et
varia repagula quibus turpe illud monstrum
pellices suas occludebat."*[1]   After Freydier,
Dulaure has somewhat embellished this
passage. He asserts what Misson does not
say, but merely hints, namely, that Francesco da Carrara's acts of cruelty brought
him to the scaffold: that one of the charges
taken up against him was, that he put padlocks and girdles of chastity on all the
women in his seraglio; that a chestful of
these tools was preserved long after they
had served as so many convincing proofs
at the monster's trial. A desire of getting

---

[1]   "There, too, are padlocks and several kinds of
safety-tools with which the fool monster was wont to
secure his concubines."

some particulars about so singular a trial
and so accomplished a mediæval tyrant very
naturally led us to make inquiries; and great
has been our disappointment, indeed, not to
find any, or to find such facts as are in com-
plete contradiction with the assertions of
Misson, Freydier and Dulaure. The Italian
chronicles collected by Muratori speak
nearly all of them at great length of Francesco II da Carrara; for he acted a notable
part towards the close of the 14th century;
and he was really strangled in his prison
at Venice, but only as a political enemy,
because he seized upon Verona and a few
Lombard towns, at the death of Galeaz Vis-
conti. The Venetians retook Verona from
him, then blocked him up so closely in
Padua, that famine compelled him to capi-
tulate. They proposed to give him sixty
thousand gold ducats and let him quit the
town with his whole household and as much
of his furniture and goods as he could con-
vey in one day, on condition, however, that
he should leave the seigniory of Padua to
Venice and live afar like a quiet private
gentleman. Carrara consented at first, then
altered his mind, saying he wished to die
Lord of Padua; he made a last effort and was

obliged to surrender at discretion. The
Council of Ten, after holding him a few
months in custody, had him strangled with
two of his sons, prisoners like himself, for
the peremptory motive, "that a dead body
wages war no more"; these are the very
words of one of the judges; and a rumor
was spread among the people that he died
of a catarrh. His trial and execution are
described with full particulars by Andrea
Navagero[1] Sanuto[2], by the author of
"Chronicon Tarvisianum" and especially by
Andrea Gattaro[3]; there is not a blessed word
about his seraglio, his padlocked women,
the strange chest that killed Countess Sacrati
or his pocket cross-bows. The historian of
Padua gives on the contrary the following
description of the monster: "The said Seignior Francesco de arrara was a stout well-
shaped middle-sized man of dark complec-
tion, rather haughty in his look, discreet in
his conversation, gracious and gentle with
his people, merciful to all, very skilled in
sciences and fearless for himself." He does
not look much like a man who kills people

1) *Storia della Republica Venezia.*
2) *Vite dé Duchi di Venezia.*
3) *Istorio Padovana.*

for fun. Abbé Misson must have lent too
complaisant an ear to the stories of some
sophistical cicerone. There, then, remain
only those padlocks and boltworks which he
must have seen and the existence of which
appears to be certain, whether they come
from Francesco da Carrara or somebody
else. When President de Brosses visited the
small arsenal of the Palace of the Doges,
less than a century after this traveller, those
tools were reduced to only one, and the
tyrant's seraglio, decreased in the same proportion, was composed of not more than one
woman, his lawful spouse. "It is likewise
there," says the witty President, "that there
is a celebrated padlock which once a certain
tyrant of Padua used for securing his wife's
honor. This woman must have had a great
deal of honor, as the lock is extremely
large[1]!" That is how legends vanish, when
we look a little closely into them.

As President de Brosses did not think
proper to describe this padlock for us, and
as Abbé Misson's modesty kept him from
saying any thing but a few words in Latin
about the ones he had seen, we can only

---

1) *Lettres familières*, XVIe.

surmise what they were like. Fortunately,
we know the diverse systems employed in
the framing of those ingenious apparatuses,
both from precise descriptions, and the specimens now extant in public collections.
The simplest is that of one of the girdles of
chastity preserved in the Musée de Cluny,
Paris (fig. 1). The occlusion is formed by
an ivory beak fastened with a lock to a steel
hoop provided with a rack. The ivory beak,
whose curve follows that of the pubis and
nicely fits into it, is furrowed with a longi-
tudinal cleft for the passage of natural se-
cretions. The rack permits the hoop to be
fitted to the waist; the hoop is overlaid with
velvet, so as not to wound the hips, and it
is held at the required notch by a turn of the
key. A tradition, unjustified by facts, af-
firms that this girdle is the one which Henry
II put on Catharine de Medicis; its smallness
would never permit one to fit it on a woman
with so rich an embonpoint as the queen,
to whom a soldier gave the answer related
by Brantôme. She asked why had the Hu-
guenots christened a huge culverin after
her: "Madam," said the soldier, "it is because its caliber is larger and stouter than
all the rest."

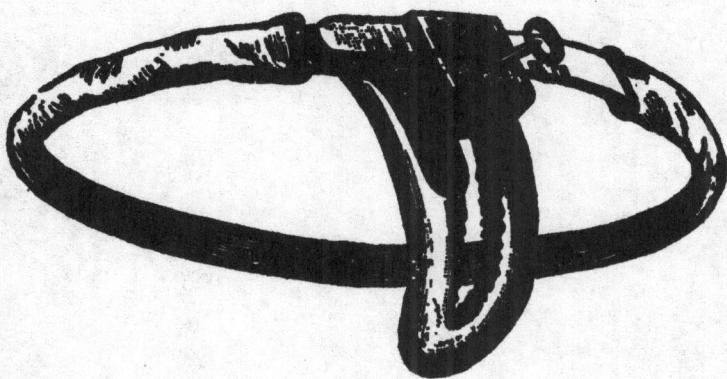

FIG. I

Henry II was the first to use this peculiar instrument of torture. He had it devised for Catherine de Medicis as a little token of his love for her. That it acted as a preventative was probably a mere coincidence. Later he discovered that there were upwards of three hundred keys in current usage. Hence the saying; "Love Laughs at Locksmiths."

Nicolas Chorier, in the work above quoted, describes a girdle of chastity resting on a different combination over the pubis by four chais, two of which, welded to the top of the grating, are fastened to the girdle before; two more are fastened behind on pass-

ing under the thighs. Our readers will be
thankful to us for giving here the passage
which contains a full description of it:

Ottavia. I heard my mother saying something or other to Giulia a few days ago about
a girdle of chastity. But I do not know how
this girdle can make women chaste.

Tullia. Thou wilt learn it. Next day,
when Giulia was getting up, Giocondo
drew nigh. Once the witnesses were out of
sight, he displayed the famous belt. She on
laughing: — "What is the meaning of this
thing thou hast there, whereon I see shin-
ing gold?" she inquired. — "Thou wilt
please put on this girdle of chastity, this
very instant," he replied, "in order to preserve thee from the maternal blemish. They
call this thing a girdle of chastity; my mistress, Sempronia, wore it several years before thee; it is now thy turn to clap it on.
Owing to it she won her high reputation; I
hope thou wilt acquire as good a one." The
gold portcullis was suspended by four little
iron-chains overlaid with velvetings and rivetted with similar art into a belt of metal
to match. Two of the chains on one side and
two on the other held up the girdle by being
passed through it behind and before. The

girdle was fastened behind above the hips
by means of a lock adapted to a very small
key. The portcullis, being about six inches
high by three in width, thus ran from the
perineum to the edge of the outer lips; it
covered the whole space which extends between the two thighs and the bottom of the
uterus. As it is formed of three open bars,
the urine finds an outlet, whilst it refuses
an entrance even to the tops of one's fingers.
Thus that part is protected as it were by a
cuirass against foreign mentules; only he
to whom the law of Hymen allotted has an
easy access to it whenever he chooses.

Ottava. What must the bride have said
to herself?

Tullia. What thou thyself wilt say in a
few days, because they are also preparing
a similar kind of apparatus for thee.

Ottavia. I was not aware of what Caviceo
was up to when he said, concerning the
girdle of chastity, that it was the surest de-
fense of honest women's virtue, and when
he asked me whether I would be willing to
put on one as my mother would advise me.

Tullia. "What must I do?" asked Giulia,
whilst her husband was throwing aside the
bedclothes.—"Put," said he, "one foot into

these two chains and the other into those."
Both feet being in, he pulled up the girdle,
placed the portcullis before the slit, bound
the pit of her stomach, a little above the hips,
with the girdle and locked it. "Now," said
he, "thy pudency is secured; it is all right,
but wilt thou think hard of wearing it?"
—"Certainly not," she replied. Thereupon,
he bid her rise naked, get out of bed and
walk about. She rose as she had been
ordered, jumped out of bed, and advanced
a few steps; she said she could not walk so
readily as before, being obliged to spread
out her legs owing to the huge size of the
portcullis. — "Never mind," said he, "thou
wilt become accustomed to it; I do not won-
der at thy not feeling at ease, this being new
to thee."

5

But no: all was not yet safe, no more with this system than with the previous one. The grating of gold, like the beak of ivory, protected only the chastity of the fore part, while leaving the other wholly undefended. A Frenchman might put up with it; we are

therefore inclined to believe these tools are
of French manufacture; but an Italian of
the 16th century (let us spare our contem-
poraries) would have never thought his
wife entirely safe with so incomplete an
apparatus. The jealous husbands of that
time were too suspicious, too well up to the
habits of their countrymen, to secure but
one side.

The second girdle preserved in the Musée
de Cluny answers much better the double
object that the Italians were to propose to
themselves, and it is exceedingly worthy of
note: excellent as a preservative, it is at the
same time an object of art. It is composed
(fig. 3) of two plates of forged iron, engraven, damaskeened and pinked with
gold, united at the bottom by a joint, and
at the top by a girdle of wrought iron.
There are holes made all around the edges
of the plates and girdle for linings to be
sewed on. The front plate, which the position of the object in the glass-case scarce
allows one to see, has a notched aperture
of an elongated form at its lower end; the
aperture in the back plate is in the shape of
a trefoil. Both are decorated with masks and
arabesques; but the figures of Adam and

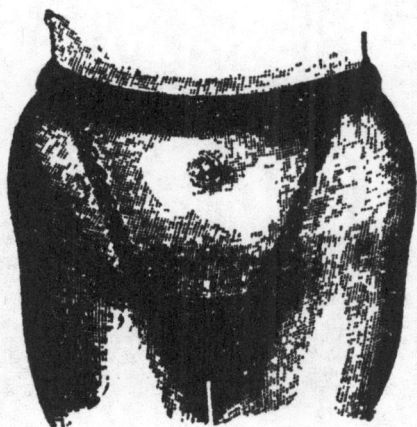

FIG. II

The daintiness of the girdle pictured above was
motivated by the asceticism of the first Crusaders.
When they departed for the Holy Land, they en-
trusted the keeping of the keys to an ancient,
feeble man. By some strange turn of fate, the old
ne'er-do-well suddenly amassed great wealth, and
the warriors returned to find their wives looking
much better than they should have been.

Eve are further engraven on the fore part:
on this head, we can refer the matter only
to the Catalogue. Figure 4 represents the
padlock placed behind at the side, and figure
5 gives an idea of this girdle applied to a
woman with a back view: it is a cuirass,
proof against the best tempered weapons,
and defying on each side alike the most
daring attempts. This is a thorough Italian
contrivance; and so it really is from Italy
that Meremée brought it, in order to present it to the Musée de Cluny.

The author of the article "Ceinture de
Chasteté',, in the *Encyclopédie*, describes
another with as nice a fastening, but of quite
a primitive construction. "The girdle," he
says, "is composed of two thin and very
pliant plates of iron set together crosswise;
these plates are covered with velvet. One
goes round the body, above the loins; the
other runs in between the thighs, and its
end comes to meet both ends of the first
plate; the whole three are joined with a
padlock of which the husband alone knows
the secret spring. The plate that runs in
between the thighs is bored so as to make
a husband easy about his wife's good be-

haviour, nor does it derange the other
natural functions."

Must the girdle, of which Freydier speaks
in his speech in behalf of Mdlle. Lajon, be
placed among the specimens of this kind?
It was not, at all events, an object of gold-
smith's art to be compared with the one we
have described above. Freydier defines it
"drawers hemmed and net-worked with
several brass-wires united by needle-work,"
for the preservation of which there were
numerous stamps of sealing-wax on the
watch. It must not be of an examplary
solidity, despite of the lock that commanded
the whole system; Sieur Berlhe, the tyrant
of Padua of Miss Lajon, must have made
it himself of the remains of some old coat
of mail. It would be an object of only
greater curiosity for this, had they preserved it in the Museum of Nimes, as the
production of a free natural art, owing
nothing to the imitation of masters.

Every one is agreed, at least among us,
to credit Italy with the invention and more
or less common use of the girdle of chastity.
Diderot calls it the Florentine tool. Voltaire
believes that it is in general use at Rome
and Venice. Saint-Amand also says that, in

his time, most Roman ladies used to wear drawers or trowsers of iron:

> With a trowse that Crazy-Body
> With his own hands forged
> Their wives' bottom is clogged,
> Lest it should play the fool.
> *(Rome ridicule)*.

Rabelais[1] puts into the mouth of Panurge the following words: "The deuce, he that has no white in his eye, take me then with him, if I don't buckle my wife in the Bergamask fashion, when I go out from my seraglio!" This expression would lead one to believe

---

1) *Pantagruel*, book III, ch. xxvi.

that the Bergamasks used those kinds of fence still more commonly than all other Italians; or that the locksmiths of Gergamo had acquired the same degree of superiority for this style of manufacture, as the sword-cutlers of Toledo for the tempering of fine swords. We read in the *Memoirs* of Count de Bonneval, the celebrated adventurer, of his amours with a lady of Como, who chanced to have on one of these girdles. There was no means of cutting or ripping it open without it being discovered, and her life was depending upon it. Bonneval killed the husband in a duel and was obliged to fly to Vienna, where, the story having leaked out, ladies of the high aristocracy and the Emperor Francis-Joseph put a thousand questions to him about this curious tool, unknown in Austria. But these Memoirs are apocryphal. It is a pretty strange particular: the more information we find in French authors about Italian girdles of chastity, the more silent are the Italians themselves on this head. Nobody, to our knowledge, points out any allusion made to them in their romancers of the 15th and 16th centuries, so fertile withal in love stories, conjugal misadventures, and ven-

geances of jealous husbands. Let whoever
will explain this anomaly.

Be that as it may, the fashion was very
near being introduced among us in the reign
of Henry II. "In the time of King Henry,"
says Brantôme, "there was a certain pedlar
that brought to the fair of Saint-Germain
a dozen of certain tools for bridling
women's affairs. They were made of iron
and went round the waist like a girdle and
branched down to be caught at the bottom
and locked. They were framed with so
much art, that it was not possible for the
woman, once she was bridled with one, ever
to be able to avail herself of it for sweet
pleasure, having but a few small holes to
serve for making her water.

"They say there were some five or six
peevish jealous husbands, who bought some
of them and bridled their wives with them
in so safe a way that they might well say:
Farewell merry time! And so there was
one of these women who took it into her
head to keep company with a locksmith,
who was very subtle in his art, and to whom
she showed the said apparatus and her own
and every thing. The husband being gone
out to the fields, the locksmith bent his mind

so closely on the affair, that he forged a false key for it; the lady had the pleasure of fastening and opening it at all hours, and when she wished. The husband never found any thing amiss with it; so she took her fill of this fine pleasure, in spite of the jealous foppish cuckold husband, who fancied he would always live secure from cockoldom. But the roguish locksmith, who made the false key, spoiled all on him, and, according to what they say, did still better; he was the first to enjoy her and thus made a cuckold of him. They say, moreover, that there were at Court many honest gallant gentlemen, who gave the pedlar to understand in severe terms, that if ever he attempted to carry like trumperies, they would kill him; that he should not go there again; that he should throw all the others which still remained into the privy, which he did. And he was never talked of since, which was very wise of him, as it was enough to have half the world lost, for want of peopling it, by binding nature with such bridles, locks and clasps, the abominable and hateful enemies of the multiplication of mankind."[1]

---

[1] *Vie des Dames galantes;* Discourse I.

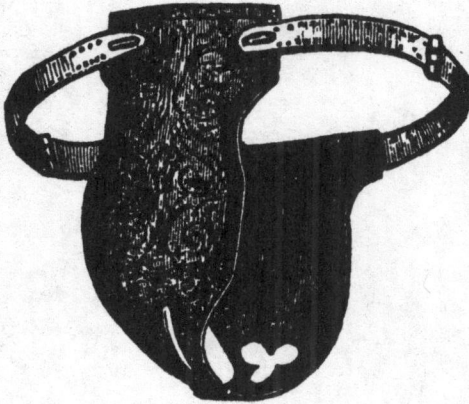

FIG. III

With this figure, things grow rather more complicated. An ideal protection against cold weather, truly, but there are other methods of gaining warmth. What has puzzled many students is the design engraved thereupon. The sages have answered that, like other inventions of the devil, it is to lure men to their destruction. After looking at the illustration again, we cannot doubt the truth of that remark.

7

The introduction and use of those tools in France would go a great deal farther back than the reign of Henry II, were we to take in their literal sense certain pretty obscure words of writers of the 15th century. Guillaume de Machault, for example, speaking of one of his mistresses, says:

> Then the fair lady hugged me . . . ,
>
> So she reached a little key
>
> Of gold, made by a master-hand,
>
> And said: "This key carry,
>
> Friend, and keep it safe,
>
> For it is the key to my treasure.
>
> I make you lord of it henceforth,
>
> And above all you shall be master of it,
>
> And therefore I love it more than my right eye:
>
> For it is my honor, it is my wealth,
>
> It is what I can be generous with . . ."

Agnès of Navarre wrote to Guillaume de Machault: "Please not to lose the key of the box I have, for if it were lost, I think I should never have perfect joy. For, by God! it shall never be unlocked by any other key but the one you have and it shall be so when you please." Guaillaume replied to Agnès: ". . . As to the key I carry of the very rich

and gracious treasure, which is in the box,
in which all joy, all grace, all sweetness are,
doubt not that it shall be very well kept, if
God is pleased and I am able. And I shall
bring it to you as soon as I can, in order to
behold the graces, the glories and the riches
of that loving treasure." Commentators
have quite simply thought that Agnès of
Navarre wore a girdle of chastity of her
own accord, in order to warrant her lover
of her constancy, and gave the key of it to
Guillaume de Machault. Monsieur de Laborde [1] denies that these passages ought to
be interpreted in this manner, and that it
would be giving them quite a different
sense to what was in the writers' minds;
perhaps he is right. In the last episode of
the *Aloysia,* of which we have given the
translation, Giocondo, after putting the
girdle on his wife, at the instigation of Sempronia, his mistress, returned to the latter
with all speed: "And now, mistress," he
cried, "I have two keys to offer thee, but
this one first" (he showed his *mentule*),
"for I can no longer bear it!" And if Guillaume de Machault and Agnès de Navarre

---

[1] *Notice des émaux du Louvre,* tome II, *Glossaire;*
art. *Trésor.*

did not speak of one of these two keys, did they mean then to speak of the other? Fortunately for Count de Foix, husband of the fair Agnès, we can still interpret these passages in quite an allegorical and immaterial sense, sufficiently conformable to the refined symbolism of Cupid's faithful.

FIG. IV

And here is a close-up of the lock. Ambitious
lovers were known to have spent months un-
raveling its complexities without notable success.
The mediaeval husbands used to meet in taverns
for the purpose of gloating. The only satisfied
lovers were those of the plumbers' wives, whose
mates were in the habit of forgetting their keys.

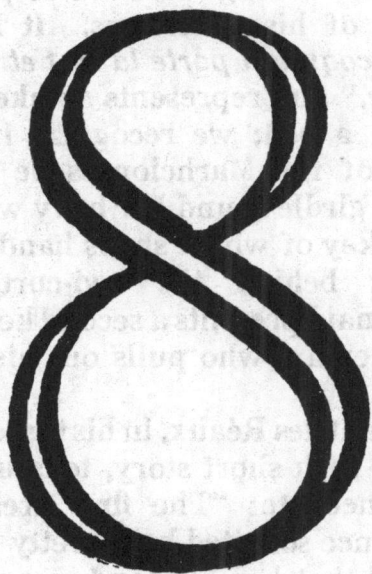

From the close of the 16th century to the middle of the 18th, indications about girdles of chastity, though not very numerous, give all the same to understand that the pedlar of Brantome did not cast all his wares into the privy. Monsieur Niel, in his Portraits *du*

XVIe siecle, names a satirical picture from
which we may conclude that Henry IV was
suspected of taking this kind of precaution
with one of his mistresses.   It bears this
title: *Du coqu qui porte la clef et sa femme
la serrure,*[1] and represents a naked woman
seated on a bed; we recognize in her the
features of the Marhcioness de Verneuil.
She has a girdle round her body with a padlock, the key of which she is handing to the
Bearnese; behind the bed-curtains, the
chambermaid presents a second key to a gallant gentleman, who pulls out his purse to
pay her.

Tallemant des Réaux, in his three hundred
and forty-fifth short story, tells us the following anecdote: "The first president Le
Jay was once solicited by a pretty lady, who
pretended that her husband was so jealous
that, when going away, he had put iron
drawers on her.   This inflamed the president: the drawers were not so tight that they
could not be drawn back; but the good man
caught a milchcow with her.   It was a trick
they were playing on him." In the language
of Tallemant des Réaux, a milch-cow sig-

---

[1]   Of the cuckold who carries the key and his wife
the lock.

FIG. V

This shows the rear view of a girdle used by the second Crusaders. They were not quite so trusting as those who went before. When they left their homes they gave their keys to another old man. Some of the fighters, with visions of oriental beauties in their minds, told the old man to throw the keys away. Others, lean and restless instructed him to exchange their keys for *different* keys, in the hope of finding more delectable entrances upon their return.

nifies, by a pretty smutty metaphor, a ven-
ereal running; that girdle was then a very
scurvy jest. The one which they assert that
Duc de Centadour bestowed on his wife was
of the same suspected nature; we are therefore somewhat surprised to see the following lines[1] under the signature of M. Gustave
Brunet: "All persons knowing any thing
about the intimate history of the Court of
Louis XIV are aware that the Duc de Ven-
tadour, a very ugly deformed man, married
Mdlle de la Motte-Houdancourt, who was
much talked about for her beauty and in-
trigues. Madame de Sévigné relates the sly
saying of Madame Cornuel about the report that spread concerning the measure
taken by the duke to baffle the projects of
his spouse's adorers: He has put a good porter at the door!" The erudite bibliographer
believes that this porter was of iron and
came from the ironmonger's. Not in the
least, and you will be convinced of it when
you read Madame de Sévigné's sentence to
the end: "Madame Cornuel says that the Duc
de Ventradour has put a good porter at his
door ...' by giving his poor wife a fine dis-

---

[1] *Revue archéologique*, vol. X, 1853.

ease." He had, then, made the unfortunate duchess the same kind of present as the solicitress made the good man Le Jay; this, still less than the anecdote of Tallemant, has no connection with girdles of chastity.

When Voiltaire was a young man, he had an opportunity of seeing and fingering one, which was quite authentic and solidly bolted round the body of one of his first mistresses, whom he designated by the still mysterious name of Madam de B....; it is what won the nice tale of the *Padlock* for us. The author, says a note in the Kehl edition, was about twenty years old when he composed this piece of poetry, addressed in 1716 to a lady against whom her husband had taken this strange precaution; it was printed for the first time in 1724.

Girdles of chastity were not, then, of such rare use as we might be tempted to believe at rst sight, and we find another proof of it in the speech of Freydier, lawyer at Nimes, in behalf of an unfortunate girl whom her lover compelled to encumber herself with this portable prison, whenever he went on a journey. This speech is previous to 1750, in which year it was printed for the first time. In order to be well acquainted with the matter, we would want the rest of the brief, the speech of the adverse party and especially the judgment, the clauses of which could not fail to be of curiosity; but the harangue of the Nimese lawyer has alone been saved from oblivion. A Nicolas Chrorier would have perhaps turned this smutty cause to a better account; still, this performance, such as it is, deserves to be appreciated by connoisseurs. At all events, it is the last positive document we have on this matter; it closes the series of information that can be gathered together concerning a custom which is very likely altogether out of use to-day.

SPEECH OF MONSIEUR FREYDIER ON BEHALF OF MADEMOI·SELLE MARIE LAJON VERSUS SIEUR PIERRE BERLHE PRISONER OF THE COURT

THE present action has no precedent in the amorous Annals of France. Hitherto we may have seen enterprising crafty lovers ruin simple young girls, and then add perjury to seduction, ingratitude to outrage. We may have also seen weak credulous females, who, after sacrificing their honor to the flattering hopes of a suitable match, found them-

selves betrayed and driven at last to wear
out the remainder of their days in shame
and wretchedness. But, Gentlemen, I may
tell you in the present cause you will find
pieces of singularity, that heighten and
place it beyond the domain of ordinary
rules.

On one hand, we see a raw young girl,
seduced by the artifices of a base ravisher
and the hope of a speedy settlement; we
see her carried away from the midst of her
kindred; taken by her lover to several
places; disguised as a man by the very fellow whose slave she has become.

On the other hand, we see a man of an
age when human passions rule with sway.
This man, after having used the most un-
remitting seduction to triumph over the
young girl's virtue, was not satisfied with
being master of her mind and heart: he
was still cruel enough to bring her body also
into slavery, by attaching to it a *chain-
padlock*, or *girdle of chastity;* for the purpose, no doubt, of gradually introducing
among the French a barbarous custom,
which rank jealousy had until then suggested only to the Italians and Spaniards.

Such are the various traits that go to

characterize the guilt of Sieur Berlhe. Were
there ever any more deserving of punishment in this matter?

I shall give you now, Gentlemen, the
abridged plain history of Mdlle Lajon's misfortunes; and, though she speaks here only
through my ministry, yet her modesty and
heart are greatly pained at the recital. It
is a sad thing for a young girl to see herself
compelled to avow her frailties, and to bring
to trial, he who was once the object of her
attachment. It is a painful thing for her to
be in the dire necessity of loading him with
cruel but just reproaches, and of calling
him by his name.

Yet, what did the young lady (whom I am
defending) not do, in order to bring the un-
grateful fellow over to his engagements?
She tried for a long while with tears and
sobs to remind him of his protestations;
she repeated his promises to' him a long
time, but it was all useless to a heart given
up to inconstancy and levity. She finds herself, therefore, forced to load the false fellow with confusion, and to call on him the
penalties he deserves; as the only way to
reclaim him, Gentlemen, is to engage all
your severity against him.

Mdlle Lajon is from the town of Toulouse. She went to Montpellier some time ago to see her relations on the mother's side; thence she proceeded to Avignon to live with her brother who is settled there, and who was then lodging in the house of Sieur Berlhe. The latter had occasion to see this young girl, who is pretty liberally adorned with the gifts of nature. At first, he had a certain propensity for her, but he contrived to hide it with such courtesy as decency seemed to authorize.

Mdlle Lajon was not over susceptible of impression then. So she perceived undisturbed the apparent civilities of Sieur Berlhe. Her heart quietly at rest, she was awaiting her parents' orders. Meanwhile, the young man leisurely improved the opportunities that the circumstance of their living under the same roof afforded him. He slily paid her his most earnest addresses, and grew distractedly fond of her. Yet, he contrived to play the counterfeit, lest Sieur Lajon, who was more clearsighted than the sister, should discover the drift of his assiduities.

However, this kind of restraint served but to excite the desires of Sieur Berlhe. He

let no fair opportunity slip without compli-
menting the young girl on her charms. He
would cry up her graces at one time, and
at another show off to her his assiduities
and wishes.

Now, a young girl of Mdlle Lajon's cast is
easily persuaded. Being herself incapable
of deceiving any one, she naturally sup-
poses every body else has a similar character, because honesty attends this state of
early innocence.

With Sieur Berlhe it was quite otherwise.
With a mind fertile in expedients and the
most proper means of deceiving, he artfully
declared his love to the young lady. He
called God to witness his tenderness for her.
He made her promises and oaths. In a word,
he tried all that is most dangerous in the
fatal science of loving, and most studied in
the art of seducing.

Such language was new to Mdlle Lajon;
it alarmed her modesty. But Sieur Berlhe
gained her over to such extent, that she did
not distrust a man, who was giving his
courtship the appearance of a merely lawful end. Ah, fatal credulity! Unlucky bait
with which young girls let themselves almost always be caught! That was exactly

the trap set by Sieur Berhle and Cupid.

Meanwhile, Mdlle Lajon gave ear to those entreaties with a kind of security, and ascribed to them only a purely upright motive; because her early innocence bore her up still. Owing to the facility he hed of seeing her at almost every moment in the day, he padded, as it were, all the roads to seduction. He feigned so much simplicity and candour, that she had no diffidence of him.

Girls are frail and unaware of danger. They expose their virtue imperceptibly. Wooers, on the contrary, are cunning. And there are critical moments when bold enough to venture every thing, they are only too sure of getting all.

Sieur Berlhe, by continually repeating his oaths of Mdlle Lajon, got her to believe in the sincerity of his promises. One day above all others, unlucky day that was the source of all the young girl's misfortunes! —she can not think of it without shedding floods of tears; one day Sieur Berlhe said to her: "Thou oughtst not to doubt that I love thee to madness. I swear to thee that my mouth is the faithful interpreter of my feelings. I assure thee I shall never have any spouse but thee, if thou wilt only requite my love. Thou alone art the sole object of my desires. I shall be the happiest man alive, if I can gain thy affection."

Did any one ever tell his passion in more animated, more spirited or more expressive phrases? So many assurances shook the young lady's virtue at last. So many united promises, seemingly sincere though really false and artful, produced the effect that Sieur Berlhe desired. He discovered in her eyes the fatal impression his own had made in them. She felt in her turn several motions unknown to her till then. A marriage promised, and sworn a thousand times over, fully convinced her. Ah, cruel moment! A certain tremor came over her. In her uneasiness she foresaw her defeat. Yet, she still defended herself, or at least tried to do so; but her strength forsook her, and she was overcome.

That is how Sieur Berlhe availed himself of the young lady's weakness and triumphed over her virtue; and how, after adorning his victim, he sacrificed it to his inflamed desires. But, while she was still in a state that merited some little indulgence, the seducer swore the strongest oaths as fresh pledges of his tenderness and fidelity.

Mdlle Lajon having recovered, announced
her pain with her tears. She groaned; but
her wound was too deep for remedy. She
was surprised that her strength should have
forsaken her. She sought her heart and did
not find it. Vain sorrows! To listen to a
wooer is to risk every thing. By giving ear
to him, a girl insensibly falls into the preci-
pice he has dug under her feet. The flowers,
which the seducer skillfully scatters, cover
the entrance of the abyss. She finds out the
danger only when she has forgotten her wisdom and lost her maidenhead.

Thus love nips in a single instant a virtue, which is the work of several years. It
rifles a treasure, guarded till that moment,
with all possible care, a treasure whose loss
is irreparable.

Once Sieur Berlhe had executed so black
an attempt, nothing could put a stop to his
audacity. He saw the young girl frequently
and he barefacedly took all the liberties of
a husband with her. How often did he not
use the rights of his first victory?

But he had not all the freedom he desired at Avignon, because he was afraid
Sieur Lajon might in the end fathom his de-
signs and observe his courting. So he won

the young girl over so far as to prevail on
her to quit her brother's house, and follow
him to Beaucaire and to several other towns
in Province.

When a girl is once seduced, she is wholly
in the power of her seducer. He alone dis-
poses of her lot. She is no longer mistress
of her feelings or actions. As she imagines
that she can no longer expect any thing but
from the fidelity of her ravisher, the will of
the latter becomes her supreme law; so that
we ought to look upon him as the author
of all the ravished girl's frailties.

Sieur Berlhe disguised Mdlle Lajon first
as a young man; then he made her cast off
this transformation only to shut her up two
months and a half in a room at Beaucaire.
There he was plunged with her in that kind
of intoxication into which the poison of
pleasure is wont to cast the senses. There
he quietly enjoyed his crimes and mistress.

He next conducted her in the same disguise to Montpellier, to Saint-Gilles, to several other towns, and finally to Nimes.

In the latter town Miss Lajon found out
she was with child. She informed her lover
of it. She urged him not to put off their
settlement any longer. But he sought va-

rious pretexts to elude the fulfilling of his
promises: now his business obliged him to
postpone it; now it was a journey. He did
indeed go on a journey; but on the eve of
his departure he compelled his mistress to
let a *girdle* with a *padlock* be put on her. We
shall describe this hereafter.

What used Mdlle Lajon to oppose those
delays? Sieur Berlhe knows very well. She
opposed to them with tears and sorrow, sorrow for having given herself up to a cruel
perjured man.

He came for her some time after, and
brought her back to Beaucaire, where he
confined her a second time in the same
room, which had already served for his
pleasures. In short, he took her again to
Nimes, where she was delivered of a daughter. She had no sooner given birth to the
child, than he clapped the *girdle* on her
again; she wears it still.

Sieur Berlhe was present at his mistress's
confinement. The witnesses give evidence
to *having found him by her bedside at the
time of her delivery.* But little by little he
began to loathe his love. His mistress's
charms had no longer any attraction for

him. Such is the fatal effect of a gratified passion.

Meanwhile, Mdle Lapon employed with him such means as she thought most proper to bring him over to his duty. The rascal then told her plainly, as it is shown by the inquiry, that *he was not free to marry her; that in order to do so it was necessary to wait till the death of his mother, who would not give her consent to this marriage.*

Mdle Lajon rightly regarded this delay as a fair evasion, or rather an odious pretence of infidelity. She felt in that instant the whole weight of her misfortune. She saw she was fooled by that low seducer. But she needed only her own grief to open her eyes; she lodged a complaint against him; upon this complaint a warrant was issued against him, and an inquiry was made.

Then Sieur Berlhe promised anew to marry her, for the purpose, no doubt, of putting a stop to the suit. He demanded only his father's procuration. When it was sent, they treated about the dowry. But here was a fresh pretence: the mother of Sieur Berlhe did not think the portion considerable enough. Driven to extremity by those affected delays, the young lady has resumed her proceedings and asks for sentence aginst Sieur Berlhe to undergo penalties and pay damages.

Gentlemen, such is the state of the case.

The ravisher against whom we are proceeding is a corrupter who joins guile to unfeelingness. He does not love, or more properly speaking, he has never truly loved her. All the promises he has been reminded of were but the offsprings of a brutal passion. They all ceased with it; they all vanished with the honor of her who was their object. Thus loathing always attended gratified passion; favors in this matter serve only to make villains.

Sieur Berlhe does not, therefore, trouble his head about Miss Lajon's condition or cries; for most men of the present day glory in not being chaste. They pique themselves on robbing women of their honor. They flatter them merely to ruin them; they approach them but to betray them: and then they call gallantry what the law calls a *great crime*. They regard as a lucky feat what Justinian regards as the *snares of a very wicked man*. They treat as trifling matter what the Church treats as *damnable lewdness*. So that if they have any shame, it is

of being shamed, and not let all their honor
consist in dishonoring a young girl.

Quite right, Gentlemen, that you should
not give ear to those girls who have lost all
reserve; who impudently appear before
men as if to request their defeat, who seek
it by their looks, and who go to meet
seduction.

But does not a young girl like Miss Lajon,
who has been seduced, deceived and dishonored, deserve that Magistrates should in-
terest themselves in her behalf; that they
should avenge her for such an act of per-
fidy; and that they should oblige the base
inconstant ravisher to marry her?

A similar crime, perpetrated on the person of Dinah[1], caused the spreading of dis-
order, bloodshed and carnage over a whole
Province. But if the outbreak of punishment can not be so great in our days, is it
less necessary to impose on the culprit the
pain he deserves? Was not what Mdlle Lajon lost through the seduction of Sieur
Berlhe as dear to her, as what the daughter
of Jacob once lost through the violence of
Sichem?

---

[1] *Gen.* ch. 36.

It is, then, but just to avenge her. Sieur
Berlhe, in contempt of his oaths, refuses to
keep his promises and do justice to her innocence and virtue. He ought to meet with
such rigour in a judgment for proportionate damages, as will compel him to do so out
of lucky necessity.

But as we must always proportion venge-
ance to crime, it is proper, Gentlemen, to
examine here:

1st. The characteristics of seduction;

2nd. The circumstances of the one which
Sieur Berlhe used in order to overcome
Mdlle Lajon. This examination will deter-
mine the indemnity she expects.

Seduction in general is an action through
which one draws ignorant or unlightened
innocent persons by the most plausible and
bland allurements into the ways of error
and crime. It is a piece of address on the
side of the seducer to lead those to his ends,
whom he purposes leading to them; and too
excited an inclination on the side of the seduced for an object that attracts them by
outward appearances.

The seducer's chief aim, in point of love,
is to gratify his passion and vainly by satisfying a secret and dainty longing he has to

possess what he likes. Let us now trace
the means of seduction, or rather the conditions that characterize it, and let us at the
same time apply them to the case.

The first condition necessary for seduction is, that the person seduced or ravished
be a minor and younger than the seducer.
Now, in the present case, Sieur Berlhe is
twenty-six years old, according to his interrogatory, whilst the girl seduced is not yet
eighteen, according to the indictment.

The customs of the world give men a superiority above girls. Thus Sieur Berlhe's
eight years constitute an undoubtedly superiority, especially if we observe that the
girl in this instance is naturally timid, and
even somewhat shy. She believes every
body is honest, because she is full of candor.
She is favorably prepossessed about the disposition of those that approach her, because
she herself is of an excellent disposition.

The seducer is a young man who obeys
but his passions. His propensity to liber-
tinism corresponds with the corruption of
his heart. He joins a rare audacity to his
lewdness, but the girl, whom he attacks, is
at that critical age which affords neither
sufficient strength nor thought to escape

from the perils that threaten her innocence.
She has not prudence enough to secure her
against snares and artifices; for she judges
blindly of the step taken to delude her. She
does not distinguish good from evil, truth
from falsehood, what is useful and honest
from what is not so. Her want of expe-
rience should then save as an excuse for her
weakness.

Owing, therefore, to a presumption
grounded on justice, seduction is deemed as
proceeding rather from the man than from
the woman, as it is easy to deceive and soften
her. Her heart readily yields to credulity.
The Emperor Justinian, who says he is sufficiently acquainted with women's frail nature, asserts that they are apt to be easily
deceived and seduced.

Indeed most of them yield rather through
weakness than passion. The first woman
was seduced, because she was weaker than
the man, and those of her sex have ever
since preserved that weakness. Hence, ven-
turesome men usually succeed better than
others, although they are not more amiable;
and the most fortunate lover is often he who
is most skilled in telling lies.

But if women in general deserve our in-

dulgence, how much more deserving of it is
a tender unenlightened young girl, who is
ignorant of the wiles that the passions sug-
gest, as she never has had any passions? She
does not know the shifts that the fatal
science of loving suggests, as she has never
loved. She has just come into the world,
whereas the ravisher has always frequented
it. In short. she knows neither fraud nor
guile, whereas the seducer is the man who
knows best how to practice frauds and
wiles.

Therefore the laws protect young girls
whose weakness and frailty are exposed to
men's malice. "As it is certain," say the
laws, "that those young girls are very weak
and frail, and are apt to be easily deceived,
and are exposed to the snares of men, it is
right to lend them favourable assistance and
defend them against such attempts."

"Nothing is certainly fairer," says the celebrated Cujas, "than to excuse such girls as
are engaged by men's knavery in unlawful
and ill-hatched conjunctions."

The second condition required for seduction is when the ravisher, to gain his point,
has employed graces, designing words,

promises of marriage and all that the art
of seducing is wont to use in order to de-
bauch the reason and pervert the heart, in
such a way that whatever the ravished girl
has done may be less the work of her own
choosing than the effect of an impression
and foreign violence.

The *seduction of graces* paves the way to
the others. The graces open the scene and
dispose the action. They are a sort of pag-
eant that strikes the senses and clouds the
reason. They are a kind of brilliancy that
flatters and seduces.

A seducer artfully sets off his good qual-
ities. The desire of pleasing is the very soul
of all his actions. He displays his fairest
side under an engaging aspect. Thus love
can disguise a wooer, although he be, at bottom, only a ravenous wolf seeking his prey.

Now, who would not have been deceived
by the air Sieur Berlhe most ingeniously
affected? He changed his temper, he disguised his defects and imperfections. He
placed himself in a point of view that rep-
resented him to Miss Lajon as a good friend
and guest, whereas, in reality, he sought but
to betray the laws of friendship and hospi-
tality. Yet these *graces* and first looks make

way to a young virgin's heart through her eyes, like so many poisoned arrows.

The other traits are derived from the *seduction of words*. In fact, nothing can match a seducer's eagerness, attention and civilities. He grovels in order to acquire the favors of the girl he desires. Yet he does not pursue his point at once; he goes on reducing by degrees while preparing all his springs.

An ancient [1] describes the artifices of lovers in these terms: "Their words," says he, "are but entreaties, supplications and oaths. They pursue, they besiege, they become, as it were, willing slaves."

A Father of the Church[2] marks the progress of seduction, thus: "The eye," says he, "looks and seduces the mind, the ear listens and gains the heart by slow degrees."

Indeed, a lover exhausts himself in oaths and protestations. He employs all the craft his passion suggests to him. He seems to place his heart on his lips, in his eyes, all over his frame. He disturbs, as it were, the whole firmament in order to bring it down to his compliments. What transformation he undergoes! What babble he uses to give idle fancy a look of reality, and folly some appearance of wisdom! He tries to instill into the object with which he is enchanted, or with which he feigns to be so, the tenderness that he himself shams. He is lavish of the pleasing declarations common to lovers. In a word, all that art has most engaging is put into practice. And the end of all this amorous eloquence is to seduce a girl, whom he has unfortunately chosen as the object of his seduction; so that his fair discourses are equivalent to force and violence.

In this manner Sieur Berlhe dealt with regard to Mdlle Lajon. This likeness has been copied from him, nor could it be a better resemblance. How often has he not given this young girl those titles which an ardent love inspires, or which more properly seem to spring only from tenderness? How often, in those intimate frequentations, has he not vowed to her an everlasting love by all that Religion holds sacred, and that men venerate? Those awful expressions were so many perjuries in the heart and mouth of Sieur Berlhe.

But the most specious of all the means for seducing a young girl is the *promise of marriage*, when maintained by oaths preceded by frequentations and attended with good manners. This promise completes the girl's dizziness; she staggers; and she falls at last.

What, in fact, is more enticing than a promise of marriage between persons of equal rank? The mistress yields to the lover in the hope of being soon his wife. Now, as this way of seducing is always the most lawful excuse for the seduced girl, it is also the most criminal one that the ravisher could use. For the suit is honest in its principle, and the frequentation that it determines seems to have nothing criminal about it, respecting the lawful views with which the seducer decks himself out. The deluded girl imagines that she has to expect every thing from a man, like Sieur Berlhe, who can dispose of himself and offer his hand in exchange for what he requests. This was principally the alluring bait with which Miss Lajon has been caught.

Would Sieur Berlhe pretend that his promises ought to be written? No law authorizes such an idea. The promises, which he made in the circumstances that the indictment mentions, ought to make a greater impression than a simple promise in writing. The latter may be the effect of the interested importunities of a girl, who requires it as a reward for her favous, or the terms of her fall. One may write such promises in those fits of agitation and madness, when passion can refuse nothing to come to the main point; whereas those that are made in presence of witnesses are the mere performance of a deliberate free will. Sieur Berlhe's are of the latter nature; the evidences say *that he promised Mdlle Lajon several times, that he would never have any wife but her.*

It is true he denies his promises to-day. But, besides that they are proved by the charges, will any body presume that he speaks the truth, and is faithful in his statement? What sort of sincerity and fidelity may we expect from a ravisher, who slights assurances, oaths and all that honest people respect most? From a man who trifles both with his mistress's honor, and the word he pledged her so often to marry her. From a man who is guilty to the girl he has seduced by his false oaths; to God whose majesty he has despised, by wrongingfully taking his name to witness; and to men, by breaking the firmest ties of human society, sincerity and honesty?

"I made no promises," he says but it follows from the inquiry and his own answer that he has *expressly agreed to his having kept company with Mdlle Lajon these three years, or thereabouts, and having constantly had carnal dealings with her.* Now, when this carnal connection is proved, and owned by the culprit, the promises of marriage are deemed proved; for, it can not be presumed that a girl, like Mdlle Lajon, gave herself up to Sieur Berlhe out of mere voluptuousness and from a certain disposition of temper. Had he not deflowered her and corrupted her innocence she would never have ceased to be virtuous.

The third condition of seduction exists when there is rape of the person, or at least when, pursuant to the insinuations of her seducer, the seduced girl forsakes her parents' house, in order to place herself entirely at his mercy.

Now, Sieur Berlhe used rape with regard to Miss Lajon. The indictment proves that he has agreed to his *having torn her from her brother's hands, at Avignon.*. He owned in his interrogatory, that, *being arrived at*

Beaucaire, he confined her in a room, in which he kept her two months and a half.

It would be needless to oppose that the abducted girl favoured her own rape, and that, consequently, the punishment for it should be mitigated.

The law has foreseen this shift and condemned it. For, the law, on recognizing that the ravisher holds the will of the girl he has seduced in a state of traldom, has imputed to him all the unfortunate creature's outward consents and seeming voluntary acts. It has looked upon the girl's will as the first product of subordination, a corrupted will.

"We wish ravishers to be punished," says the law, "whether girls have or have not consented to the rape; for," it adds, "it is to be borne in mind that the ravisher's seduction has swayed the will of the seduced girl."[1]

A celebrated jurist remarks that the penalty of this law exists although the girl consents to being carried off, whether she consents to it in the beginning or afterwards.[2]

"The punishment for rape," says another jurist, "exists although the girl assented to

---

[1] *Leg. unic. cod. de rapt. virg.*
[2] Jul. Clar.

her ravisher's design, and this ought to be a thing of course," he goes on to say, "when, by dint of promises, the ravisher persuades the girl to leave her parents' house to go with him; because it is an act of violence, to behave in this manner."[3]

Sieur Berlhe's seduction proved so effectual on Mdle Lajon, that it obliged her to go with him, on disguising her sex, to Beaucaire and then to several other towns. Is not this a true rape? What other definition do jurists give it, when they say that that man is guilty of rape, who leads the ravished girl about from place to place, for the purpose of abusing the power he pretended to acquire over her, and of satisfying his own lubricity?

What remains now, is to ask Sieur Berlhe: what motive was it that urged him to pick Mdlle Lajon from her brother's hands and take her to Beaucaire? What was his design in dressing her in boy's clothes? What was his aim *in keeping her two months and a half is a room at Beaucaire?* for he admits this fact. Was it to study Nature, or merely to make her produce? The girl's pregnancy,

---

[3]   Pyrrhus Corrad.

one of the first results of that cloistering,
but too clearly showed that Sieur Berlhe pre-
ferred voluptuousness to physics, and the
title of father to that of mere naturalist.

Yet, though there was not an effective
rape as to Mdlle Lajon, but only rape of seduction, it is not less punishable, since no
difference is to be made between those two
rapes.

In fact, the laws have established the pain
of death not only against ravishers, but also
against those who seduce by words and cor-
rupters of virtue. They have come to the
conclusion, that it is unimportant whether
one should use force or persuasion: because
the rape of seduction is still more dangerous than that of violence, in so far as it
causes the greatest disorders in families, by
raising children against their parents. It is,
therefore, more severely punished. The
Greek legislators, being convinced that persuasive words have a coercive power, used
to inflict a severer punishment on the man
who seduced the sex by words, than on him
who employed open violence.

A celebrated doctor,[1] writing on this ques-

---

[1] Isidore of Pelusium.

tion, expresses himself in the following terms: "You let yourselves be won over unreasonably to the common belief, viz., that the man who takes a girl by force, is more guilty than he, who drives her to crime by persuasive words. As for me," he says, "after having duly considered the nature of the case, I do believe that he, who seduces a girl by force itself, and because he, who takes the body by violence, leaves, at least, the mind pure and unaltered; whereas the former corrupts the mind, and then the body; he is therefore twice as guilty."

As this belief seems to be the most reasonable, it has been followed by the ordinances of our kings. These have expressly subjected the crime of seduction or subordination to the pain of death; because they concluded that he, who corrupts the mind and heart by persuasive discourses to gain his point, exercises a kind of tyranny for which he ought to be punished more severely than if he had made himself to be obeyed by force. In fact, he diffuses a quick poison into the heart, a poison more dangerous than death itself. The more skill he has in instilling it, the more guilty he is. The

speedy issue of his enterprise is a proof
of his malice.

Can any match be found for Sieur Berlhe
in this line? He vanquished Mdlle Lajon
by artifice and suppleness; but his victory
made him cruel. Not satisfied with having
enslaved this young girl's heart, he also
wished to put her body in irons, and thus set
up in every way for a tyrannical master,
by treating her more cruelly than if she was
a slave.

Now, what instances of a greater sway
and barbarity could there be, than to wrap
a young lady in chains? To put her body
in slavery? To confine her in a prison
which she continually carries with her
everywhere? To secure it with a *padlock*
whose structure might be left to the care of
the most jealous Florentin to imitate?

A kind of drawers, hemmed and worked
like the meshes of a net with several brass
wires woven into each other, forms a girdle
that comes round and fastens in front with
a padlock of which Sieur Berlhe has the key.
This contour, which forms the enclosure of
the prison of which he is the gaoler, has several seams which are sealed with brands of
red sealing-wax, set from distance to dis-

tance. Sieur Berlhe holds the seal with
which he makes these brands, and, indeed,
the engraving on it is most singular and ini-
mitable. But there is nothing surprising in
this: a porter usually takes his precautions,
and wishes to be sure of his gates and locks.

The whole of this apparatus is so framed,
that there is barely quite a narrow space left
open, and this is bristling all round with
sharp spikes which make it inaccessible.
Sieur Berlhe would fain have been able to
close this up too, but the needs of nature
were opposed to his doing so. And yet this
passage, notwithstanding its narrowness, is
trimmed with several impressions, which,
while corresponding in a circular manner
to one another, are like so many sentries
watching for the safety of the place, or like
so many eunuchs that are guarding the door
of pleasures, and keeping the abode of de-
lights night and day under lock and key.

Is such mechanism the contrivance of a
new beginner? Must he not, on the contrary, have fed a long time on the taste of
carnal pleasure and be acquainted with all
its circumstances, in order to bring out such
inventions and make reserves for himself
in this way?

When Sieur Berlhe was questioned on this point in his interrogatory: *Whether he set a* Girdle in the English fashion [1] *with a padlock of which he has the key,* on Mdlle Lajon, *in order to go on debauching her and prevent her from having connection with other men; whether there were several seals on this girdle, made with red wax and a seal which he carries about him an wdhich he used to compare whenever he went to see this girl; whether hè took this girdle off her at the time of her delivery, and put it back on her afterwards:*

He replied: *That he had never seen this girdle; but that, indeed, Mdlle Lajon had told him she had made one, and put it on herself.*

Were the matter to stand as Sieur Berlhe

---

[1] The Magistrate wronged the English, by calling this girdle, a *girdle in the English style.* No people are less given to jealousy. These islanders, who try to imitate the ancient Romans in every thing, care just as little, as they did, for their wives' infidelity. They imitate Lucullus, Pompey, Antony and Cato, who had gallant wives, whose conduct they were not ignorant of, and yet they did not trouble their heads about it. They leave with Lepidus alone the paltry glory of dying with vexation for it. When returning home, they send word before them to their wives; this preliminary is less a proof of their politeness than of their indifference respecting jealousy. It is then more proper to call those girdles, *girdles in the Bergamask fashion,* as Rabelais has done in tome 3, book 3 ch. 35.

asserts, it goes to show that he is exceedingly given to jealousy, and that Mdlle Lajon, desirous of freeing him from his suspicions, set herself on a kind of rack. This proceeding becomes, therefore, a proof of both of Sieur Berlhe's jealousy and of Mdlle Lajon's attachment for him. But this false allegation of Sieur Berlhe is overthrown by what results from the indictment: *Mdlle Lajon wore a girdle of brass-wire trimmed in front, where there was an iron-padlock, which had been attached to her by Sieur Berlhe, who kept the key of it as well as the seal, the impression of which seemed to be made in sealing-wax on several parts of this girdle. The said seal was indeed frequently seen in Sieur Berlhe's hands; and he stated that, though Mdlle Lajon remained at Nimes and he at Beaucaire, he was sure of her fidelity, and that she certainly could not hold any frequentations with another man, because he had provided against the like.*

How dares Sieur Berlhe be so bold then as to say he has never seen this girdle, whilst it is the work of his jealousy? How can he assert that Mdlle Lajon put it on herself, whilst he fixed it on himself, and avowed that, owing to his foresight, *he had himself taken this precaution?*

On this accoun, he did not wish to give up the seal or key, which he has even still in his possession. Therefore Mdlle Lajon has been obliged to petition you to bind Sieur Berlhe by your first command to deliver both to the clerk's office, and to have this padlock opened and the girdle taken off by two officially appointed and duly sworn midwives, who will draw up a report on them, to be joined to the charges.

This petition produced no effect on Sieur Berlhe, though he had notice of it. He was satisfied with stating in his defence, that Mdlle Lajon *wishes to have* this girdle, and he thinks this shift doubtlessly dispenses him from delivering those objects. We shall copy his own words: *Let nobody,* says he, *make a display of a certain girdle. for, besides that Mdlle Lajon* wishes to have it, *by way of a joke, she can not increase her pretended damages for that, as it can have done her no wrong.*

Now, let us explain this verb: *to wish to have.*

In the first place, *to wish to have,* means to desire something from another, as people

do not want to wish for a thing they have
already themselves. The girdle of which
there is question was then in the hands of
Sieur Berlhe, when, according to his own
words, Mdlle Lajon *wished to have* it. He
was therefore imposing on you when he
stated in his Interrogatory, that *he never
saw this girdle.*

In the second place, *to which to have,*
means to wilfully lay claim to, even to ac-
cept with a certain pleasure what is given
to us; so that *to wish to have* a girdle signi-
fies to quietly allow it to be put on, to receive it without murmuring, to consent to
it with a kind of complaisance. But is not
this same will, this resignation, or, more
properly speaking, this submission to so
wild a fancy, the very effect and consequence of seduction?

When a girl becomes the victim and slave
of a lewd man, are her thoughts free while
her mind is thus restrained? Has she liberty to act of herself, whilst, owing to the
effect of seduction, she looks upon, she
minds no law but the one which caprice dic-
tates to her master, and whilst, in a word,
she lets herself be guided by her tyrant's
will?

Is it not then quite easy to know exactly whose will it was that directed this measure? Nobody will presume it was Mdlle Lajon's. On one hand, her virtue did not require any precautions of this kind; on the other hand, she was contented with the choice which destiny had procured for her and which Sieur Berlhe had determined. She thought of nothing but of him who had her first flowers. So that, even though one should presume that she *wished for* this girdle, that she let it be put on her without sorrow or regret, it is a sensible proof that she would have considered with the same indifference whether she had this girdle, or not, as, indeed, her wisdom has never depended on bolts or padlocks.

So when this measure is attributed to Mdlle Lajon, it then becomes indifferent in itself; whereas it is far more reasonable to suppose that it was the product of some specious motive. Now, the proceedings prove that this motive was nothing else but foresight, precaution, or, more properly speaking, the jealousy of Sieur Berlhe; as he assured people, *that Mdlle Lajon certainly could not hold any frequentations with an-*

other man, because he himself had taken his precautions.

Those are precautions in the Italian way; nor will it be out of place to state here, that they are the invention of Francesco Carrara, imperial Viguier of Padua.[1] We learn from history that this seignior was remarkable for his cruelties. To add to his other crimes, he was barbarous enough to padlock his mistresses. There is a dressing-chest still preserved at Venice, in the palace of San Marco, containing several of those *girdles*[1] and *padlocks*. They were produced in the action taken against this monster as so many proofs of his guilt.

This fashion did not take at first. As Carrara was strangled at Padua by a decree fro mthe Senate of Venice, in the year ₁4U5[2], the jealous people of that time admire the invention, but they did not dare use a precaution which had cost its author so dear. However, they subsequently introduced it among them by slow degrees. Soon the number of the guilty made them so unpunished; and, at last, things came to such

[1]   Misson, *Voyage d'Italie*, tome I, u. 217.
[1]   *Ibi sunt serae et varia repagula, quibus turpe illud monstrum pellices suas occludebat.* Mison, *ibid.*
[2]   Misson, *Voyage d'Italie*.

a pitch that, according to the celebrated
Voltaire:

> Since that time, in Venice and in Rome
> There is no pedant, cit, or gentleman
> But, to guard the virtue of his house,
> Lays up a stock of girdles and padlocks.
> There, every jealous man, without fear of blame,
> Holds under lock and key the virtue of his dame.

We find in recently written Memoirs [3] the
following description of one of those mod-
ern padlocks: "It is a kind of coat of mail
shaped somewhat like the bottom of a sling,
which makes the passage impenetrable. A
quantity of little chains fasten this wire-
work to a girdle, which diversely tied ri-
bands render almost unshaken."

We read in Brantôme [1] that this precaution, which the Italians thought fit to take
with their wives, was near being introduced
into France, in the reign of Henry II. An
Italian dealer took it into his head to spread
out a dozen of these *iron-girdles* at the Saint-
Germain fair with the intention of introducing the fashion among the French; but
he was immediately threatened with being
thrown into the Seine if he carried on that
trade, and this obliged him to lock up his
goods and fly. "And ever since," says an

---

3) *Mém. du Comte de Bonneval*, tome I, page 74.
1) Brant., tome II, disc. 1, p. 176.

author,[2] "nobody in France has thought of getting these padlocks made, or of sending to Italy for them."

It then lay in store for Sieur Berlhe to make the second attempt at introducing those padlocks into France. The same motive, that induces the Italians to padlock their wives, suggested to him the idea of having recourse to one of those cumbersome girdles for Mdlle Lajon.

Such is the fatal effect of jealousy. This passion, which tortures the lover as much as the beloved object, is good only for hastening, most times, the evil one dreads. But let us see of what nature that jealousy of Sieur Berlhe is.

The Italians are jealous by nature. Now, Sieur Berlhe is from Avignon, almost an Italian town, where *Italianism* somehow reigns. It is not surprising then that this jealous temper should be found in him, and that he should really be as jealous as an Italian.

The Spaniards are jealous from a feeling of vanity and self-love, which constitutes the chief character of that nation. Now,

---

[2]   Rabelais, tome III, liv. 3, ch. 35.

Sieur Berlhe minded but his self-love, when
he padlocked Mdlle Lajon; because, in fact,
there is no passion in which the love of one's
self reigns so mightily as in love. People
are, therefore, more inclined to sacrifice the
peace of the beloved one, than to lose their
own. We may then rightly conclude that
Sieur Berlhe is as jealous as any man can
be in Italy or Spain, and that it is the spirit
of these two nations, which inspired him
with the structure and use of this padlock.

Now, if Miss Lajon yielded to this seducer's artifices and listened to the lessons
of love which he insinuated into her unex-
perienced heart, did he think she would
yield to others? Ought not this young girl's
virtue, which he found so hard to seduce,
to be secure from those wild suspicions?
Can not man be then jealous, without the
woman's being unfaithful to him? Will an
idle suspicion be a proof of the reality? Can
the virtue of the sex be preserved only in a
seraglio, or in the keeping of eunuchs and
bolts?

Frenchwomen have enjoyed their liberty till now. They have enjoyed that natural faculty, which is so amiable, so
precious, and which leaves them free to act

and decide for themselves. Shall people try
to take it away from them to-day, in order
to plunge them into slavery? Thus, they
are all concerned, you see, in Mdlle Lajon's
cause. If Frenchmen were formerly seen
to stoutly resist the introduction of a tyrannical tribunal,[1] got up beyond the moun-
tains, Frenchwomen are equally interested
to-day to battle hard against the Padlock-
fashion; for, it comes from the same direc-
tion, bearing with it the same marks of
slavery and tyranny.

They are but right to be jealous of their
liberty. Nature has been pleased to favour
them with this treasure; can they be blamed
for seeking to preserve it? Shall they, who
were born free, become slaves in consequences of love or by force of jealousy?
Their virtue is more meritorious when they
are at liberty to pursue good or evil. Shall
this virtue be made to depend henceforth
upon the force and necessity they will be in
of being virtuous? Does not liberty make
the merit of every action? What will become of them if they are deprived of it?
Bodies have their duties as well as minds;

[1] The inquisition.

virtue ought to direct them; reserve and modesty ought to form their character. It is not to be feared that, owing to the vicious propensity of nature, they might be more inclined to the things which they are forbidden?

The Italians and Spaniards make it their sole business to secure the possession of the beloved one, nor do they trouble their heads about her affection. Hence the pleasure that arises from this constraint is neither brisk nor piquant. Love often delight in frustrating their precautions; and a comic author was right in addressing them the following lines:

> O you who, with a jealous mind,
> Under lock and key hold a spouse,
> Inspite of all your bolts and your padlocks,
> Cupid, when he takes his measures,
> Will have the key of your bolts:
> This oracle is more trusty than Calchas's.

The French, on the contrary, seek to flatter the fair, and win them by gentleness. They try hard to owe the love of their wives to their own personal merit; and it is the delicacy of this feeling that seasons their pleasures.

This does not mean that there can not be jealous people every where. In Boniface

we see the follies of a Provencal[1] whose
jealousy breathed nothing but fury and
madness. We may, however, generally say
that France is a fortunate country, in which
people have at all times breathed an air of
that would be agitated and tormented with
honest liberty; a country in which women's
virtue is not imprisoned; a country in which
they are allowed on the contrary a certain
licence, that, while choosing themselves
what is good, they may also by themselves
display their honesty and merit. So that
Sieur Berlhe can not be sufficiently punished
for having brought the pattern of those
fatal girdles among us.

What displeasure would it not be for our
fair sex, had this fashion been introduced
on their account? How would they accus-
tom themselves to this restraint? What de-
spair for them to see complaisant men, like
the ones they have had till now, changed
into restless, surly, jealous fellows? fellows
that would be agitated and tormented with
such vain apprehensions as make the pur-
est virtue suspected; fellows who would
watch all their steps and proceedings. Those

[1] Boniface, tome Ier, livre 5, tit. 8, ch. 3.

jealous minds would scrupulously weigh
the words, accurately sift the slightest expressions, scrutinize the looks, even search
into the breatings of the heart. Those
strict censors those incorruptible over-
seers would look upon the shadow of evil
as a downright certainty of crime. In
short, those jealous men would, thanks to
Sieur Berlhe's fashion, introduce new expedients in the shape of bolts, gratings and
padlocks.

In this manner the Italian and Spanish
women let themselves be gradually subju-
gated by a restraint which does nothing but
irritate their violent desires. Owing to the
force of the restraint, they are in the fury
of a revolted passion. Most of them are
indebted only to bolts for their good behaviour. The padlocks, which are the nearest
vouchers for their fidelity, secure, it is true,
those women's virtue. If the restrain,
which unruly suspicions have imposed on
them, keep them from making their husbands what the latter dread to be, it is not
their fault.

In fact, the more a man affects to deprive
a woman of liberty, the more excited she
becomes to take the leap; the more she

thinks about losing a thing of the loss of
which she had got so high an idea by the
very captivity in which he holds her. So
we may say that this restraint is the stum-
bing block of the generality of those
women. Ought we really to expect meritorious behaviour from force and restraint?
If we have so much esteem for purity, it is
only for that which is free and voluntary;
because if it is the result of restraint, it is
then false virtue.

It is therefore more proper to curb the
sex, not with padlocks or material chains,
but with those of honor, by inspiring it with
the true sense of honor. Mistrustful care
does not form women's virtue; honor alone
can keep them to their good behaviour.

Besides, how can we resolve to make the
persons we love unhappy? Do people try
to please, when they compel the object of
their love to live thus in restraint? "A
lover," says Plato, "is a friend inspired by
the Gods." But, is not a lover like Sieur
Berlhe inspired by demons? Does this manner of padlocking the object of one's fond-
ness mean love? Monsieur de la Roche-
foucauld is quite right, when he says, that
natural ferocity makes fewer cruel persons

than self-love; and that if we judge of love
by the great bulk of its consequences, it
looks more like hatred than friendship.

From what source does such derange-
ment flow into the minds of this class of
lovers? "It proceeds," says the Roman
orator, "from the dread they are in lest any
body else should enjoy the same object."
It arises from the suspicion they entertain
of being paid in the same coin with which
they often pay other people. They are
changeable, and they suppose the same
change exists in others. So, to obviate the
consequences of this inconstancy, they have
recourse to padlocks, without ceasing for
all that to be inconstant and fickle themselves.

Such has been the exact conduct of Sieur
Berlhe with respect to Mdlle Lajon. The
various circumstances, which I have been
relating, characterize his crime, and they
ought to determine the pusishment he deserves. He is guilty at once of rape and seduction, but of a seduction which has had
singular consequences. It is fit then to examine the penalties that attend them.

The ravisher was condemned by the law,
which was given to the people of God, to

marry the ravished girl, whether she was
rich or poor.

The laws of Lycurgus and Solon left the
girl her choice between the death and the
marriage of her ravisher. The Athenians
acted in the same manner.

The Romans, those master of the world,
used to condemn the ravisher to death, and
they would not even allow him to marry the
ravished girl to escape this death.

The ordinances of the Kingdom are not
less severe. That of Orléans commands
ravishers to be sued at law, without paying
regard to the letters of pardon they may
obtain. That of Blois "requires that those
who may have debauched a girl under age
of twenty-five years old, under promise of
marriage or other pretence, without the
assent, knowledge, will and express consent of fathers, mothers and guardians,
should be punished with death without hope
of pardon; notwithstanding any consent
that the girl may have given before, at the
time of, or after the rape."

The disposition of these laws was re-
newed by subsequent ordinances. The ver-
dicts of the Supreme Courts, which con-
formed to the general law of the kingdom

as far as it punished the ravisher with death, are to be had in every compiler of Decrees.

The object of this punishment is to allow fathers and mothers to continue their authority over their children and hinder them from deviating from their duty. Rape is a crime quite opposed to public honesty and to the peace of families, which it concerns so essentially that children should not be led, by a crime so hurtful to civil society, into mismatched and almost always dishonourable marriages.

But God forbid, Gentlemen, Mdlle Lajon should urge the pain of death passed on ravishers against her lover! Let him live, but that it may be to make amends for her honor; let him live, but that it may be to put a stop to her tears. It is then the part of justice to pass a sentence on him, as being guilty towards her, for such considerable damages as will impose upon him the salutary constraint of fulfilling his engagements.

He himself agrees to *having kept company with Mdlle Lajon for about three years; he does not deny that he is the author of her pregnancy.* Is there a better proof than the one that comes from the prisoner's

own confession? In short, it is proper that
he should be sentenced to pay damages.

Now the circumstances ought to settle
these damages; and you ought, Gentlemen,
to grant such ones as the young lady, whom
I am defending, has sued for in her petition.
First I showed that she is worthy of the protection of the laws; that a promise of marriage was the principal cause of her fall.
This object was not above her hopes, there
being no disproportion in the age of the
parties. Their fortunes are the same; their
conditions are alike; and, if we go back to
their parents and ancestors, we find them
all on the same level.

Damages are due in proportion to the
wrong one does to any body and to the injury he suffers from it. Now what greater
injury can one do to a young girl than to
rob her of her honor? What has she left
when she has lost her virginity? Her virginity is a priceless treasure, as it is indeed
the most lasting glory, and the most essen-
tial portion of a Christian girl.

In fact, virginity procures for a girl what
she must receive only in the next world. It
becomes virginity alone to symbolize and
closely represent on this earth, which is but

a place of mortality, the immortal life. In short, virginity is the first of the states of life; it is the ornament of morals, the holiness of the sex, and a beautiful flower that should be dearly and preciously preserved.

Mdlle Lajon has lost this flower through Sieur Berlhe's artifices; this flower which is nothing else but the life of honor, a life infinitely more precious than that of nature. Had Sieur Berlhe taken away this girl's life, what would she have lost but what she is to lose one day quite naturally by the law common to all mortals? But when he ravished her, he took away from her what death itself could not have wrested from her. She exists indeed, but she is as if she were dead. She is a girl, but she is no more a virgin. She has lost what she had most dear to her, and this loss is of such a nature, that it can not be received.

The Scriptures say that the Virgin of Israël is fallen, and there is nobody that can raise her up again. Saint Jerome, writing on this subject, makes no scruple of saying that, although God is omnipotent, yet he can not restore a girl's virginity once she has lost it, or decorate her with the flower which was snatched from her.

Infamy is one consequence of this loss, owing to the shame that men have attached specially to the weakness of the sex. So, when a girl is unfortunate enough to have lost her virginity, it is all over with her; there she is dishonored; nobody looks at her any longer but with disdain and contempt.

Gentlemen, is there any indemnity proportionate to such a loss? The damages, that are granted to a disgraced girl, serve somehow only to reveal her fault to the whole universe; because her unfortunate adventure is announced in a tribunal whose sentences are passed but to be published. Therefore, only the fulfilment of the seducer's promises can, according to men's judgment, efface such a stain; and on this very account, the damages ought to be very considerable, in order to oblige Sieur Berlhe to marry Mdlle Lajon.

The quality of the parties, their birth, their fortune, the merit of Mdlle Lajon, the very conduct of her lover, all should induce him to this settlement.

But this is a ravisher of quite a new cast. He owns the courtship and frequentations; he does not deny he is the author of his mistress's pregnancy; and yet he will not fulfil his promises.

He is guilty, since the seduction and rape are proved, nor does he blush. He is troubled more than ever by the stings of his conscience, and yet what a show of safety about him!

In short, he breaks his oaths; he trespasses against the laws; he makes a young girl wretched, and all that is but jesting in this ravisher's mind. He jested when he was seducing, and he seduced but for jesting. Let us apply to him then that passage of Scripture in which the Sage, speaking of the silly excuse of him who betrays the laws of friendship, makes him say, when he is convinced, that *his knavery is only a joke*.

But since when do people look upon the severe disposition of the laws as jesting? Since when do they treat the confusion that a ravisher spreads among civil society as a joke; the disgrace he brings upon a family; the sad condition to which he reduces a young girl whom he has dishonored, even before her age permitted her to appear in the world?

Several various interests turn up in this cause. That of the honest liberty of

women, attacked in the person of Mdlle
Lajon. That of the public of which the seduced girl is a member. That of her parents, towards whom Sieur Berlhe has become guilty by carrying off this girl. In
short, that of the plaintiff who has been
deceived and dishonored forever. She
spends her days in sorrow and sadness since
her fall. Painful thoughts incessantly beset
her with all their horrors since Sieur Berlhe
affects to have wholly forgotten her; and
her lover's infidelity has given her such
grief that her health, youth and beauty are
wearing fast away.

She is, Gentlemen, truly worthy of pity
and commiseration; yet she remains continually plunged in this state of humiliation.
People bestow pity upon her, perhaps even
praises, but all this does not alter the situa-
tion. Nothing can change this unfortunate
girl's sad lot while the base fellow will not
remember his former oaths, and while he
refuses to fulfill his engagements: so that
all things invite and conspire, Gentlemen,
to determine you to strike the insensible
fellow's heart with the thunder of a severe
sentence, in order to bring him back to his
duty.

THE END